THE TOP 10 WAYS TO GET RICH IN 2021

An Entrepreneur Shares Proven Methods to Make Money

Z.Q. MITCHELL

Z.Q. MITCHELL

Printed in the United States of America
First Printing 2021
First Edition 2021

ISBN: 978-1-7364683-1-9

10 9 8 7 6 5 4 3 2 1

Thanks Momma (Cooky, yes I'm talking to you) for continually supporting me through all things no matter how rough they got for me. Furthermore, I thank you for supporting each of my ventures (the e-com stores, the YouTube channels, the game development company, and the others) This book is just as much from you as it is from me.

TABLE OF CONTENTS

INTRODUCTION

I don't care who you are, how wise you think you are, or how good of a person you think you are. At the end of the day, your wealth determines your lot in life. If you have no money, then you have no voice. If you don't believe me, then let's take a gander at one of the greatest authorities knownto man, the bible. Ecclesiastes 9: 13 - 18 (KJV) properly illustrates this point. In these verses, there's a poor man who goes above and beyond to save the whole city. He's poor, so his words were despised, and he was completely forgotten after saving everyone. Hmm... Would things have been different if he was wealthy?

Want more scripture as proof? Let's move on to Proverbs 19: 7 (KJV). All the brothers of a poor man hated him and strived in all their efforts to stay away from him. Wow! What more needs to be said after this scripture? It sucks to be poor.

Okay, back to the present: "High-Value Man" is a term attributed to a man who has his stuff together. This concept has become widespread due in part to Kevin Samuels, Image Coach & Consultant. One of the six(6) attributes, according to Kevin Samuels, of the aforementioned male is to make at least 10k per month. This equates to being called a "6 Figure man". Notice that 10k is the start! You're just getting your foot in the door at this level.

As we all know, a man is prided by his resources. This is not intended as any slight against women, and I'm just establishing the mainstream consensus concerning how vital money is; besides, money is a vitality. It dictates where you live, the foods you eat, what clothes you wear, the cars you drive, your health care, your dental care, and nearly every other aspect of your life. In summary, the more money you have, the potential for a higher quality of living. So it's incumbent upon all of us to achieve a life of financial freedom to experience the life we dream of.

So, how can one position themselves for financial freedom? It's just a slim chance anyone can achieve the wealth they desire by working for someone else. So.. that leaves you with one option, be your own boss.

By being your own boss, you have options. Maybe you want to create a separate source of income to pay off a few bills? Or you want a life of luxury. Whatever your reason, there are a lot of means to make revenue online.

Be careful, though - some of these methods can be harmful as there are many scams or other illegal activities out there.

But the truth is, there are real ways to earn wealth online - millions of people are doing it every day.

From freelance digital nomads and savvy marketers to aspiring entrepreneurs, there are plenty of business ideas to try at home with your laptop and a reliable internet connection. So, let's have a look at some genuine ways to make money online.

CHAPTER 1

START AFFILIATE MARKETING

If you are looking for a way to make money while you are sleeping, affiliate marketing might be the best choice for you. It is considered among the oldest marketing practices. You simply gain a commission if someone purchases a product on your recommendation. Let me also tell you that affiliate marketing is one of the cheapest marketing ways since you don't have to manufacture or sell a product. You only have to build a link between buyers and sellers and take your commission if a sale is made. Several online companies offer affiliate programs, and you have most probably heard about some of them. It is a passive income source, and you need to be patient, choose attractive products, and attract the targeted audience by using several traffic sources if you want to become a successful affiliate marketer like Hieu Nguyen. He is a Vietnamese affiliate marketer who was initially a software developer. In 2018, he built his first websites and sold one of them for more than 17,000 dollars. Hieu mostly builds Amazon niche websites. After working as a software engineer for two years, he realized that he didn't want to live a boring life. In June 2017, he found a local Affiliate Marketing course and built two niche sites with his content. He went on to learn how to find easy-to-rank keywords, outsource content, and build backlinks. Now, I will tell you how affiliate marketers like Hieu become successful.

Deciding on your niche

First of all, you need to find out which affiliate products you are going to sell. Let me tell you that you should choose a niche and try to influence your audience. I would suggest that you stick to one niche and generate revenue from it. You need to understand that the wrong niche can ruin your marketing efforts. The question is, how do you find the best niche for your affiliate marketing efforts? Just like all other successful affiliate marketers, Hieu suggests that you should do a short self-assessment. Find topics that you are passionate about, and figure out if people search for your chosen niche. Then, you need to understand whether the demand for those products will stay consistent or not. Other factors to consider are understanding your competition and searching for affiliate programs that work within your niche. You can also get help from tools like Google Trends.

Research on affiliate marketing programs

After choosing your niche, it is time to determine which affiliate marketing programs can help you promote your products. After all, you will earn money by advertising those products. These programs are websites that act as middlemen among manufacturers and affiliate marketers. Amazon Associates, ClickBank, CJ Affiliate, and ShareASale are some of the best affiliate networks out there. Let me tell you that these sites provide more data on how well a specific product sells, and this data can help you increase your profits.

Build your platform

You need a place to advertise your affiliate products, right? Running paid ads and making sites such as marketplaces or blogs are the two most popular ways to promote your affiliate products. First, we will discuss how to build your website as an affiliate marketer. There are plenty of options available out there while you are building your website. The easiest way is to use WordPress. After building your website, upload engaging content, and promote your products. Or you can also start a blog to promote your content. On the other hand, the best way to run paid ads is to create an engaging Facebook ad campaign.

Making money with affiliate marketing

After you have successfully built your platform and joined an affiliate marketing program, it is time to understand how to make money. First of all, you will have to create top-notch content. Most beginners try simply to publish random content and add affiliate links. However, this strategy might not be effective. You need to ensure that your content reaches the target audience. In this way, you will be able to reach people who want to buy your products. Using high-quality content, you will help people discover the right product for them. Think about it; if someone realizes that they need a specific product after reading your articles, the chances are that they will buy those items through your affiliate links. In simple words, you are helping them make a buying decision and navigating them to the site to purchase the item. Let me tell you that your articles must target investigational intent keywords. These are the keywords that people use on Google to search for the product they need. After figuring out the right kind of content, look for topics that revolve around your target audience. It is important to understand where you insert your affiliate links. After all, it doesn't make sense to insert a link at the beginning of your article before you have even explained to your visitors what benefits they will get from this product. So, wisely choose where you are going to insert the affiliate link. Add your links to appropriate places, and if your article is too long, try to insert it in the first half of your article. And make sure that your affiliate link is easy to notice. For this purpose, you can use inline banners, sidebar widgets, or floating bars. Hieu says that one of the mistakes that people make is assuming they need to increase their traffic to make more money. However, it does not work that way. You need to increase your conversion rate. Imagine if you could send more visitors to the product website! You can create a popup campaign and showcase campaigns when users are most likely to make a purchase. Studies have shown that the best time to show an ad is when a visitor is about to leave the website. It is also important to identify your highest converting content. After identifying it, make sure to make display of more affiliate campaigns on this content.

CHAPTER 2

WRITE A BOOK (EBOOK)

Writing a book is probably the easiest way to make money if you know how to write engaging and useful content. You might have thought if writing a book is worth the time and effort. Let me tell you that if you know how to make money from your books, you can make even a million dollars from your book. First of all, you need to understand that nowadays, authors need to market their books. This indicates that you should be good at marketing, as well.

Moreover, I would suggest that you write an eBook if you are planning to write a book. In the past, people believed that we could not make money from eBooks. However, let me tell you that people are actually making money by writing eBooks, and some of them earn around $500/month.

How Cori Carl and his wife earn $500 per month from just one eBook?

This American couple was looking to move to Canada. However, Carl and Casey could not figure out what the immigration process it. They wanted a book or a guide to walk them through everything. The couple searched for a manual out there but could not find anything from Amazon or library services. They could find 600 books on Amazon dealing with maple syrup; however, they couldn't find a book about immigration to Canada. Eventually, they started searching the process on the internet. Here's the lesson you need to understand; the couple found everything they were looking for, but the information was scattered all over the place. If you are going to write an eBook, you need to gather this information in one place. Coming back to the story, Carl and Casey also had to translate difficult formal jargon. After spending hours on the internet, they finally completed the immigration process and set up their new house in Canada. They had found a problem that other people might also face, and they thought of making money from this opportunity. The couple decided to turn all the information they had gathered into an eBook. They had two goals in their mind- creating a guide that will help other people with the immigration process, and an average person can understand the eBook. Fast forward a few months, and Carl and Casey are earning 500 dollars per month from this eBook. The couple only turned their research into an eBook.

How to write your book?

Before I tell you how you can earn money from your books and where you are going to sell them, it is important to understand how to write a book. I will guide you on how to write and make money from an eBook in seven easy steps.

Step 1:

You are ready to sit down and start writing your eBook. What to write about? Well, this is the first step; you need to find content for your eBook. Let me tell you that if you are writing a book, there would be publishers and editors determining what you can publish. However, this is not the case in an eBook. You can write about anything in your eBook. And that is one of the reasons why I would suggest you go with an eBook. You just need to figure out what you know, and others might want to know. For instance, you might have a secret dog food recipe.

Step 2:

If you want to write an amazing eBook that is going to help you earn more money, you should write a catchy title. Think about it, and it is the most visible thing about your eBook. If you create a catchy title and design an amazing cover, you will probably draw more buyers.

Step 3:

After you have figured out the title of your eBook, you need to map everything out. Create an outline of your eBook, and for this purpose, you can create a list of all important facts, talking points, introduction, and conclusion. For inspiration, I would recommend you to check the table of contents of bestselling books in your niche. And another way to create an outline is to list down all the highlights from your content research.

Step 4:

For me, this step is the most important one. You have to create a writing schedule and stick to it. You need to decide how much you will spend on your book each day and set a date for completing the book. If I was writing an ebook, I would write it between 10 pm, and 8 am. Why? Because most of the other people in your house are asleep and there will be fewer distractions.

Step 5:

After writing the book, edit it like a PRO. You might think that you can hire an editor for this purpose. However, let me tell you that editing the book yourself is the cheapest, easiest, and most effective option. You can even use some tools such as Grammarly, etc., to make sure your work choice is correct.

Step 6:

You also need to design a cover. If you are a very creative person, you can design it yourself. However, I would suggest that you hire a freelance graphic designer.

Step 7:

The next step involves formatting, pricing, and an enticing description. You will have to convert your eBook into the Kindle format. Discussing the price, most people prefer eBooks since they are cheaper. Although you can sell your ebook at any price, the average spot on Amazon is around $0.99 to $2.99.

Making money from your books

There are several ways you can earn money from your books. I think the best way is to sell your eBook on Amazon. You can also make money through affiliate programs and selling ads, which we cover elsewhere in this book.

CHAPTER 3

BUILD A MONEY MAKING BLOG

Blogging is another way to make money online and build your online presence. Undoubtedly, a person can make millions of dollars online if he is willing to put in the effort and stay consistent. The best part about creating a blog is you can earn money from various sources. For instance, you can promote your affiliate products, sell your own products, advertise products of other brands, and sell ads. If you have the basic knowledge of SEO and blogging, you can start your blogging business today. It requires hard work and consistency. You need to understand that millions of people try to earn money from blogging. However, not everyone can make a substantial income from a blog. Let me tell you that you must be passionate about writing if you want to run a successful blog. Ryan Biddulph is a successful blog and says that you cannot monetize your content if you are not passionate about writing. Let me tell you that this blogger writes about how to create content and monetize it. Ryan was born in New Jersey and ran a blog called Blogging from Paradise. This blogger loves traveling and shares his travel experience on his blog. After Ryan graduated from high school, he tried several jobs, and at one time, he was working as a security officer. At that time, this man decided that he would do something that would provide him the satisfaction of being free. Ryan eventually decided to start blogging. His blog is now among the most popular blogs in the world. Ryan also teaches how you can manage a blog. Here is how you are going to launch the next TechCrunch or Mashable!

Pick a topic

Just like affiliate marketing and dropshipping, choosing your niche is also an important step if you are going to launch a blog. You need to get clear about what you are going to write about. Is it related to your personal experiences? Or are you going to teach people through your blog? Regardless, the first step is to define a niche and create your content around that niche. It will also help you build digital products that complement the content of your blog.

Choose a platform

Although WordPress is considered the largest platform for blogging, you can also try micro-blogging platforms such as Medium, Blogger.com, and Tumblr. However, I would suggest that you go with a self-hosted WordPress installation on a custom domain. With a self-hosted domain, you are likely to get more traction.

Pick your domain name

If you want to make money out of your blog, it is essential to wisely pick your domain name. Your domain name should be descriptive of your intended niche or topic. And I would suggest that you try to avoid relying on a third-party-hosted subdomain. There are several domain name providers, including BlueHost, 1 & 1 Hosting, and HostGator. Expert bloggers like Ryan recommend using a top-level domain such as .net or .com. Moreover, you need to keep the domain name short. Ryan says that the domain name should not exceed fifteen characters.

Start publishing content

By this time, you will have set up your blog, and you are ready to publish your first article. Let me tell you that you can only make money from your blog if your content is outstanding. I think the most challenging part of building a money-making blog is creating the content of your blog. However, as I already mentioned, if you are passionate about writing, then it will be a fun task for you. Most people think that great content is just words. However, it can also be infographics, videos, and pictures. Pictures and videos will help you engage your audience, but your content needs to be primarily words to achieve high rankings on Google. Your blog will surely be successful if your content is unique for your site, free of grammar and spelling errors, unbiased, insightful, meaningful, and people can easily read it. Moreover, your blog should help your readers do or understand or learn something.

Build organic traffic

Let me tell you that organic traffic is generated from Google, and it will help you make money. When a person searches for something on Google, they have a clear intent. This means that if you are advertising a product or service on your blog, it is more likely that they will buy from you. If you want to build organic traffic, your content should be great, you should get your technical SEO correct, and your on-page SEO needs to be correct. Moreover, you will also have to work on your off-page SEO.

Build your community

Once traffic starts flowing in, it is time that you build a community around your brand. You need to understand that the first step is to gain users' trust before making any sales. Now, you need to think of your blog as a business. You need to have a unique logo or a unique slogan for your brand. If you successfully create a community that follows your blog, you are more likely to earn money by selling them something. You can build a community through email marketing, social media marketing, replying to comments, and web push notifications.

Start making money

Now, we will discuss the most important part of your blog. We assume that you have successfully accomplished previous tasks, now you are eligible to make money from your blog. The best way is to use Google AdSense and sell ad space. Let me tell you that the money you make from Google AdSense depends on the placement of ads, organic traffic levels, and the number of available advertisers for your topic or niche. Another to start earning through your blog is by selling your products.

As you have to build your community and your visitors trust you, you can start selling them your services or products. Or you can also insert your affiliate links in your articles. The key is to build your community, and once people regularly start visiting your blog, you can earn money.

CHAPTER 4

Become A Facebook Ads Expert

There are more than 2.23 billion active Facebook users per month - the keyword is happening there. So this number does not contain any inactive, abandoned accounts. That's 2.23 billion people who can see and interact with your Facebook ads and business!

Brand awareness and loyalty through Facebook ads can lead to better customer relationships, more sales, and lower overhead costs for your business.

When you put all of this together, you have great potential for growth at a low cost. Suppose you compare social media's price to other traditional forms of advertising like billboards, television advertising, etc. In that case, you will find that the cost per result on social media is infinitely lower.

Facebook Ads

Facebook ads now come in different flavors. You can promote your Page, posts on your Page, user-taken actions, or your website yourself. Despite Facebook's increasing focus on native ads and website traffic, you can still drive people to your website.

There are also several ad formats, including pictures, videos, carousels (multiple images), instant experiences, and collections.

How to create the perfect facebook ad?

If you've tried to market something online, you've probably tried to create a Facebook ad. But what makes the perfect ad? Of course, this does not only apply to Facebook. It applies to all paid marketing platforms.

What's the best way to design or create that perfect ad that not only appeals to your target audience but also makes them stop scrolling, clicks your ad, and eventually capture that lead and turn it into a paying ad? Converting customers; It's the look-hook-take method.

The Appearance

It stands for the image that will help someone stop in their footsteps. It should get their attention. We quickly scroll through our news feed, wait for something to appear, and grab our attention. Kusmich says to disrupt the scroll. Do this by highlighting your photo. Change images. Switch to grayscale if you need a different image or use another portrait that interferes with the scroll pattern.

The Hook

You have to hook the prospect and establish a connection. Most people want to connect with someone or something. If you can't embed them or click, you probably can't convert that prospect from a browser to a buyer. Try to develop a relationship with your ad. Use the feel & find method described earlier. Doing so puts you one step ahead of the competition.

Facebook Ad Content

The most important part of a Facebook ad is the content. Once you add an attractive image to the ad, the user will stop once but will not respond if they cannot find useful content. Hence, the priority should be to put quality content in the ad. Good content is the one that communicates the idea briefly and makes the user curious to follow the ad link. If the user clicked on the ad and reached the landing page, you're halfway there.

Create The Selling Mechanism

The next step in your effort to monetize your ads is to create a sales mechanism. Yes, I'm talking about the sales funnel. What does this mean? Just that: it's the process of finding a potential customer and bringing them into your ecosystem, and eventually becoming a customer.

Fifty percent of all people who inquire about something buy it within 18 months.

Maybe not necessarily yours. But from someone who sells it on the market.

15 percent of that 50 percent buy within the first 90 days.

What can you make so that the people who buy not only know you but love or love you enough to buy directly from you?

Your goal is for the relationship you have developed to become a transactional relationship when the potential customer is excellent and willing to buy a product, service, or information.

Who Is Your Targeted Audience?

We know that the more money you spend on Facebook ads, the more reach your ads will get. But who sees them? Are you reaching the right target group?

When customers from different marketing agencies come to us, you will be amazed at what we see in their ad accounts regarding the audiences they target!

Facebook offers a variety of targeting options! Everything from demographics, as we just mentioned, to buying habits and self-identified interests.

The Hidden Value Of The "Like"

One last little Facebook ad nugget I want to share with you that most people don't know about ... Did you know that as an administrator of a Facebook Page, you can serve ads to anyone who likes your Page? Finds?

Using one of the examples above, Straub can place ads targeted at over 5000 Facebook friends. That's cool for a couple of reasons. By serving ads to your fans, your messages can stand out from the crowd.

What's even cooler is how cheap it is to do this. You can probably get your ad to reach 1000 of your fans for around $ 1 to 2. It is challenging to get your marketing message to so many of your customers/fans for so little money!

The Sum-Up Of It:

Facebook is evolving every day to provide its users with the best possible experience while staying connected to the people around them and the people they left behind in schools and colleges. We hope you are now ready to go live with your Facebook ad campaign and start making money from Facebook ads.

CHAPTER 5

CREATE A DIGITAL COURSE

People go online for a variety of reasons, including entertainment and socializing. The Internet is the modern medium for the sake of learning new things. Not sure how to use new software?

Its need for information and instruction created an excellent opportunity for you to get paid for your knowledge. While some people have done this by blogging or writing books, taking an online course is another way to sell what you know. According to Global Industry Analysts, online learning is expected to exceed $ 240 billion.

Many people think they don't know enough about a topic to teach it, but the truth is, you don't have to be an expert to create and sell a course online. You just need to know more than most.

How To Create An Online Course

Follow the steps below if you are ready to dive into the world of online teaching.

Select A Course Topic

List the things you know. Your friends and family may be asking for help. Maybe it's a skill related to your job (using Evernote or being productive at home). Do you have a hobby that you can teach others about?

Do Market Research

You don't want to spend a lot of time creating a course that no one will buy. Many people may want to know more about your topic, but the question is, are they willing to pay to learn? Before investing time in your course, find out who the best buyer is for it and whether they are ready, helpful, and able to buy it.

Sketch Your Course

Once you have determined that a market is ready to buy your course, the next step is to decide what to include in the system. Due to the nature of a time, the content you provide should go deep into the topic and cover all essential aspects. A time is not like a blog post that often glides across the surface.

When organizing your course, think of modules and lessons. A module would be the complete sub-topic, with the classes containing the details on that topic. For example, if you have a course on starting a private business, you might have a business plan module. Your lessons in this module include "How to Identify Your USP" and "How to Identify Your Target Market."

Determine The Best Methods To Deliver Your Lessons

Online courses are expected to offer various teaching methods such as Text, video, worksheets, checklists, infographics, audio, and anything else that provides information.

The trick is to figure out which format is best for what you want to learn. In some cases, you can offer two teaching methods. For example, if you have taught a course on using Quickbooks, you may have step-by-step text instructions and a video tutorial to install and set up the software.

Decide On How You Want To Sell Your Lesson

For the most outstanding possible control, create a website to host and teach your lesson. There are scripts for membership sites and WordPress plugins that you can use to set up a system for selling and delivering your course.

For faster and less technical effort, you can use an online course service such as Udemy or SkillShare. The pay for these websites varies. For example,

Udemy's instructor salary depends on how the sale came about (through their marketplace, an affiliate, or directly from you).

Upload Your Course Online

Once you've selected your platform, upload your course. If you can customize your time on the forum adds a logo or color scheme, add them.

Market Your Course

Even if you use a service like Udemy, where students can find you in the Udemy marketplace, you should be doing your marketing.

First, create a marketing plan that outlines who your market is, where to find it, and how to get them to advertise your course. Great course marketing options include social media, PPC advertising like Facebook ads, and article marketing. There are many other free and inexpensive marketing options, as well.

Keep Your Course Information Up To Date

Check every few months that your course information is current and relevant. Out of date information does not help your students and can lead to low ratings. Don't forget to review and fix broken links to resources.

The Benefits

Various new online course platforms are available to set up and sell your course more comfortable than ever. Thanks to continually evolving technology, many of the tools and equipment required to create a system are very easy to use and produce professional results.

You can create courses for sale to complement your existing business. For example, if you're a blogger, you could offer a system that delves deeper into specific topics in your blog's subject area. By providing a service, you can design and deliver an online course for people who prefer to learn and do the job themselves rather than keep you busy.

One of the creative ways to use an online course for marketing purposes is to use it as part of a funnel system to direct students to your coaching program or another service. You can give them a small amount of information or teach them some basic service and then lead them to your other paid offers when they want more of what you have to offer.

Sum-Up Of It:

Creating and selling courses online can be very lucrative if you offer a great system and can achieve your intended marketing. Since it is easier and cheaper to host your design, there is no reason not to become an online course instructor. While it can take time to create all of the lessons in your system, once uploaded, it can become a good source of passive income for your existing business or as a stand-alone business.

CHAPTER 6

SELLING YOUR ONLINE ASSETS

You need money, infrastructure, endless partners, and a lot of common sense to build an asset. Digital products remove most of these barriers.

You don't need a factory or logistics partner; you only need yourself.

Likewise, you can teach online courses so that others can benefit from your wisdom. Whether your superpower is cooking homemade meals, setting up strenuous fitness routines, starting businesses, creating design assets, or tackling self-improvement projects, you can teach others to do the same.

Building An Online Asset

Building an online business takes time, and many online companies such as blogs, eCommerce websites, and YouTube channels are unlikely to make big bucks immediately.

You may have to work for the company for 6 to 12 months (or more) before you can start making money. You don't make a lot of money for your efforts at first, but you do so in hopes of a future payout. However, after a while, your business will gain momentum.

Traffic is increasing, and you don't have to spend as much time getting visitors, new income opportunities arise, and growing income. At this point, your hard work has paid off.

As an online business owner, you also have two options that are not always available with some other types of ancillary issues.

You can outsource the work to other people and run your company somewhat passively. You probably still need to be involved, but you can hire others to do much of the day-to-day work and turn your business into an asset that primarily makes money off the autopilot.

You can sell your business if you are ready to make money and move on to something else. Many people and companies are looking to buy a business online, and you could potentially make a few years in profit if you are ready to sell.

Why Sell An Online Asset?

To answer that question; there are several reasons you might want to sell a profitable online business.

Time Restrictions

While you can outsource much of the work associated with running an online business, there is some degree of commitment that you should do unless you have a highly skilled person whom you fully trust in running the business to run.

In other words, if you outsource most of the work, the company is likely to need some of your time and attention. We all have a limited amount of time available, and focus becomes an issue too.

When you're trying to do different things (like running multiple businesses or doing a full-time job with a few websites right next to it), sometimes selling is more effective, and you have one less thing to do.

LACK OF INTEREST

Over the years, you may no longer be interested in the subject or enjoy running the business. It's perfectly normal for our interests to change over time.

I prefer to work on things that I like. If my interests change, I can try to sell them.

SELLING HIGH

Most businesses have a finite lifecycle, and this is especially true for online businesses. If your business is doing well and is high in value today, there is no guarantee that its value will last or increase. You could see the company's value dropping significantly.

If you have been in the online marketing world for a while, you may be familiar with Digg.com.

Digg was a top-rated social media site over a decade ago. In 2008, Digg was involved in talks with Google about a reported $ 200 million acquisition, but

the deal never materialized. Digg fell in popularity, selling for $ 500,000 in 2012.

Types Of Online Resources

Niche websites

A niche website is simply a website that is very focused on a particular topic. For example, you can have a dedicated website about camping, running, wedding photography, or any other specific case.

Most niche websites are monetized through affiliate programs and display ads, but there are other options.

Blogs & Authority Websites

Blogs also tend to be more likely to engage with readers. Niche websites generally get most of their traffic from Google searches, but blogs tend to build a relatively loyal following that leads to repeat visitors.

The terms "blog" and "authority website" can generally be used interchangeably (unless you are talking about a personal blog). These types of websites are also perfect for selling. Most of the work involved in running a blog, including writing, can be outsourced, making it easier for buyers and investors.

Amazon FBA

In recent years, the demand for eCommerce companies selling through Amazon's FBA program has grown enormously. These companies can be ideal for buyers because most of the work is outsourced, and they can be scaled very efficiently.

However, selling on Amazon also involves some risks. Amazon can close a seller account at any time or make other changes, such as increasing costs.

A business can be more valuable by selling through its website or other eCommerce sites rather than relying solely on Amazon.

SaaS

Software as a Service (SaaS) companies are ideal for selling, as buyers love the recurring monthly or annual revenue generated by the subscription-based model. It provides extra stability and predictability and can add value to a company.

E-commerce

An e-commerce store is also a great option if you are looking for some type of business to sell later.

However, selling a stock business is more complicated than selling a 100% digital business.

Either way, eCommerce stores are always selling. You can find numerous examples on sites such as Flippa.

In some cases, the buyer has an agreement to purchase the remaining inventory as a separate transaction. It is done to keep the marketing and the business's sustainability in the interest of both parties.

CHAPTER 7

EMAIL MARKETING

Let me tell you that the most powerful tool to make money online is your email. YES! You heard it right. Many people think that social media, SEO, or paid search advertisements are the best ways to advertise your products and make money. However, experts believe that you can surely become successful if you do email marketing the right way. You might be surprised to know that email marketing has the highest conversion rates as compared to any other channel. Experts say that this channel is 40 times more effective at acquiring new clients as compared to Instagram, Facebook, or Twitter. Bryan Harris is an email marketing expert, and he created a list of email subscribers. This email marketing expert created a super course and had more than 13,000 subscribers when he launched the course. By selling them a value-rich course, he was able to get people to pay more than 800 dollars. In simple words, Bryan took feedback from his email subscribers and upgraded his course. In this way, he was able to get over 220,000 dollars in sales in ten days.

If you want to make money through email marketing, here are some ways to monetize email marketing.

Targeted list

Now, you are going to start your email marketing campaign. You need to start by creating a targeted email list. One of the best and easiest ways to do this is to convert visitors to your website into subscribers. You need to make your visitors signup for your email list. Successful email marketers like Bryan use an exit-intent popup to turn visitors into subscribers. When a person is about to leave your website or open a new tab, this popup will appear on their screen.

Set a goal for your campaign

Why are you running this campaign? What is your specific goal? It can be to increase sales, attract your existing subscribers' attention after long inactivity, or you might want to segment your subscribers to send more targeted messages. After you have set your goals, it is time to move to the next step.

The headline of the email

Now, you will start drafting your email. What is the first thing you notice about an email? Yes, it is the subject line. If your subject line is not compelling enough to make your subscribers read the entire email, your marketing campaign has already failed. The headline should be so strong that people cannot ignore it. You need to keep in mind that the subject line will decide whether a person will open your email or delete it.

Create an engaging email

You have successfully written a strong subject line, and the next step is to write an engaging email. Bryan says that you need to use persuasive writing and ask the reader to take action. Moreover, try to keep your sentences and paragraphs short. In this way, your readers can easily understand your message. Let me also tell you that the tone of your email should build a connection with your readers. You can do this by making use of first-person while writing the email. Another way to build a connection is to use the reader's name. In the end, the email needs to be relevant and precise. Keep in mind that your readers don't have enough time to read those long emails. And to create a great email, you should use an effective design. The email needs to look professional.

Sell your products

After you have successfully created an engaging email, it is time to discuss how you will make money through email marketing. If you don't already have a product or service to offer, this is your first towards building your fortune through email marketing. Bryan was able to make money because he had an amazing course to offer. Your product can be a physical one or a digital one, and you can also offer a service. Think about it, if you don't have any product or services to promote, what will you do with your email subscribers? If you don't have any idea of what to promote, let me tell you that you can get started by promoting an ebook, online courses, classes, workshops, or training guides, etc.

Sell other people's stuff

What if you don't want to sell your own products? Well, you can become an affiliate and promote the products and services of other businesses. In this way, you will receive a commission if a sale is made. Now, I will give an example of an affiliate connection. Suppose an online business is offering an SEO course to people. You are the affiliate, and you will help this business reach more clients. If you sell the course to your email subscribers, you will receive a commission. However, let me tell you that you need to have a strong relationship with your email subscribers if you want to monetize email marketing by becoming an affiliate marketer. Several companies, such as AWeber and ClickBank, offer affiliate programs.

Upsell premium or exclusive products

You can also offer additional products or services to your subscribers. Suppose that you are selling a course to your subscribers. Once you sell someone your course, you can offer them a one-on-one coaching session. In return, people will pay extra money to get this individualized attention.

Send and follow up

You have successfully created an engaging. You have decided what you are going to sell to your readers. You have the list of your email subscribers. Now, it is time to hit the send button. You might think that your job is complete. However, let me tell you that people might not take action just by simply reading the email.

You need to followup. I would suggest that you send out a quick follow-up email to your subscribers after two or three days. It will act as a gentle reminder and increase the chances of subscribers taking action.

CHAPTER 8

Create An Online Store

Another way to start earning money is to sell products. For this purpose, you need to build an online store. There is a growing trend in online shopping globally, and there are countless opportunities for you to make money by selling your products online. The most important step towards building a successful online store is to choose the right product. If the demand for your products is high, there are greater chances that you will become successful. And let me tell you that there is no better time than now to get started with your online store. Think about it, people are staying indoors to avoid being infected by the virus, and most of them purchase things online. Now, we will discuss how you can set up your online store.

Choose a niche

What are the products you are going to sell? Is your product a necessity or a luxury? And who is going to sell to? Some people don't put a great deal of thought into deciding their niche. However, let me tell you that this step decides your success. The niche can impact several things, including the sales figures, whether you will have repeat clients, and how much effort you will need to put into your customer support. The niche can be broken down into three parts, including price, market opportunity, and target audience. Discussing the price, you might think that the best way is to sell cheaper products. However, let me tell you that the Average Order Value gets smaller in this case. I would suggest that you price your products at 100 dollars or above.

Let's assume that you make 20% on all the sales, which means that you will make $20 if you sell a $100 item. You also need to consider brand loyalty. In simple words, you should always avoid niches that are already dominated by household names. For instance, you will probably buy Beats or Bose if you need a new pair of headphones. On the other hand, you will simply google 'purchase chandeliers online' if you are looking to jazz up your living room with a chandelier. The next step is to choose a product that is slowly but steadily growing in popularity. After you have decided what you are going to sell, choose your target audience.

Choose a business name and register a domain name

It is important to be careful while choosing your brand name. A great business name is one that is easy to pronounce, related to your niche, and unique. Moreover, the name should have an available .com domain. On the other hand, I would suggest that you avoid long names. Your brand name should be 1-3 words MAX, and it should not be a combination of words and numbers.

How to choose a product?

Now, you have your niche, business name, and URL. The next step is to figure out what you will sell. Obviously, the product will be related to your niche. But you need to figure which products are trending. Go to Amazon's best-seller list, and look for those items that are most well-received. Moreover, you can also visit eBay's best-seller list.

Look for your suppliers

After choosing the specific products, look for your suppliers. You can find numerous suppliers on Alibaba and AliExpress. Or you can also look for local suppliers.

Ensure the quality of products is amazing, and the purchasing price is low, so you can offer your customers a reasonable price while also getting your profit.

Create your website with an online store builder

There are plenty of platforms that can help you create your eCommerce store. One of the most popular platforms for startup businesses is Shopify. Go to this platform, sign for your account, choose a theme, and upload your products. After uploading your products, fill in other pages, and check over your settings before publishing your online store.

Market your store

You have set up your company and your online store; it is time that you create a marketing plan. If you are willing to spend some money, you can hire a marketing agency. Or you can also do it yourself. For this purpose, try social media marketing. Create your online presence and raise awareness about your products. Initially, you can offer your products at discounted rates to boost your sales. Email marketing and influencer marketing are some other ways to advertise your products and boost your sales. I would also suggest that you create a blog. Think about it, blogs are free to create, and they are just sitting online, waiting to be discovered by your potential customers. Let me tell you that studies have found that 38% of marketers think that blogs are the most important content for them.

The founder of Quadlock wanted to mount his phone to his bike and ended up starting a successful online store

In 2012, a man named Chris Peters founded Quadlock, an eCommerce company offering mounts that let customers attach their smartphones to a car, arm, or bike. By using their mounts, you can use your smartphone hands-free. While you are cycling or simply running, you can easily use Google Maps. Chris also wanted a similar mount that would help him use Google Maps and navigate around the country. He had moved to Sydney and is an avid cyclist. New in the area, Chris used Google Maps to navigate around Sydney. However, it was challenging for him to mount his phone to his bicycle. He could not find a reliable product on the market, so he decided to create his own mount. Ultimately, Chris funded it on Kickstarter and later launched it on Shopify.

According to Chris, we should focus on selling products instead of obsessing over beautiful themes for your websites. I would also suggest that you focus on offering value and boosting your sales. You can start with something standard and track everything from the start. In simple words, you need to build high-quality products and customer experience.

CHAPTER 9

CREATE AN APPLICATION

Create an app

You can make millions of dollars or even billions of dollars from apps. Imagine if you create an app that becomes the next Snapchat or Instagram! During the first of the year 2019, Sensor Tower reported that spending on Apple App Store and Google Play Store reached 39.7 billion dollars. We all know that people are spending more time indoors due to the pandemic, and smartphone app usage has surged, which means that creating an incredible app is another opportunity for you to make money. Several businesses are also looking to expand their business through mobile apps.

How to create an app?

The first and most important step towards making money from an application is building an incredible app. It would be best if you had a good idea for your app. If your app is useful or people find it entertaining, they will download it, eventually increasing your income. What if you don't have an idea for your app? Well, I would recommend that you think about a problem you have and then come up with a solution. Think about it; if millions of people are facing a problem and you provide a solution through your app, you can easily make millions of dollars. Or you can release an improved version of an app. Let me tell you that Instagram was released since the founders loved the filters of Instamatic. However, they thought that the app could be better if users could share photos. I am sure you also have an account on Instagram, right? Here are the steps to build your own app.

Step 1:

Plan your mobile application. You need to write down the exact idea of your app and the problem you are going to solve with your app. Moreover, figure out the target audience and choose a monetization strategy. The last part of this step is to choose whether your app will be free or paid. If you see most of the similar applications are available for free on Google Play Store and Apple App Store, it would be difficult for you to charge for your app.

Step 2:

Start building your app. There are two options. You can build it yourself, or you can use an app builder. If you don't have experience in developing apps, you might want to use an app builder.

Step 3:

The name of your app should be a clear and catchy one. The name should reflect the major functions, and it is important to include keywords in the name.

Step 4:

You should also provide a meaningful and informative description of your application.

Step 5:

After creating the app, you need to test it. Before publishing the app on Google Play Store or App Store, test it on numerous devices to see if it works properly. Moreover, get reviews from your people who fit your target audience. You will find some problems during the process; make sure to fix those issues before releasing the application.

Step 6:

While you are publishing your app on any app store, you should upload eye-catching screenshots. For instance, if you have developed a game, make sure you provide screenshots that display your game's best features.

How to make money from your app?

After you have created your app, the next step is to make money from it. After all, your primary goal is to earn money, right? There are five different monetization methods.

Paid Apps

The simplest way to earn money from your mobile app is to create a paid app. in this way, you are charging money from people for downloading the app. However, you need to offer a lot of value if you want to make your paid app a success.

Subscription

You can also charge a recurring fee from users to use the app. This monetization model is common with software as a service app or those applications providing access to media. For instance, Spotify or Netflix.

In-app purchases

The most effective ways to make money from apps are in-app purchases. Users can purchase additional options or items that enhance their experience.

For instance, games such as PUBG and Pokémon Go offer users to buy items that improve the gaming experience.

Advertising

Let me tell you that smartphone advertising is a massive business right now. Free apps usually use advertising. And you can also offer a paid version of your app, which won't display ads.

Affiliate Marketing

With this type of marketing, you will advertise products on your app, and if someone makes a purchase, you will receive a commission. Comparison or booking applications usually use affiliate marketing to generate revenue.

How Chad Mureta came up with the idea of the Fingerprint Security Pro app

Previously, Chad was a real estate agent, but an accident changed his life. This man was returning from a basketball game when an accident occurred, and Chad was hospitalized. In the hospital, he noticed doctors looking through his smartphone. Chad thought about security and started downloading applications during his spare time.

He wanted to understand what made people download some specific applications and why some of those apps were successful. Mureta sketched his idea on a paper and sent his idea to an app developer. Chad had no background in technology or app development; this man's strengths lay in the business and creative side of things. Chad submitted his app to the app store and made 12,000 dollars within the first month of release. He went on to launch his own company. Later, one of Chad's apps averaged 30,000 dollars each month. His company's income reached 120,000 per month, and Chad created and sold three application companies within the next two years. He says that 80% of business is the owner's psychology, while 20% is the skillset. Today, he leads the App Empire, which helps people turn their app ideas into successful businesses. In the end, let me tell you that the iOS and Android markets are getting bigger, and TechCrunch estimates that the market will be worth around 6.3 trillion dollars in 2021.

CHAPTER 10

START A YOUTUBE CHANNEL

Undoubtedly, you can turn YouTube into a career-building platform. We have thousands of examples in which people made millions of dollars just from YouTube. However, before you rush to this video-sharing platform to create your own channel, you need to understand your channel must provide engaging content. After all, if your videos are not engaging and do not get views, how will you earn money. Now, I will not tell you how you are going to create a channel since signing up for a YouTube channel is as easy as signing up for a Gmail account. You only have to sign in to YouTube using your Gmail. The important part here is to discuss what type of content is popular and how you can make money from your videos. Moreover, we will also discuss some strategies to grow your channel.

Popular content on YouTube

If you ask me what sort of content is popular on this platform, I would say that anything interesting and engaging can make you famous on YouTube. You must be passionate and creative. Think about it; we watch a wide range of videos on YouTube, right? However, I would still like to mention some of the most popular video categories on YouTube. These categories include singing, teaching, tutorials, fashion advice, make-up tutorials, cooking videos, pet videos, comedy videos, tech videos, product reviews, and vlogs. Moreover, you can also try unboxing videos, shopping sprees, prank videos, and parodies, etc. Want to know how some of the most successful YouTubers make money? Well, the answer to this question is pretty simple. Such YouTubers choose their favorite niche and try their best to produce quality content. We can list a thousand YouTube channel ideas; however, none of that means anything if you don't have an interest in that area. You need to figure out what YOU are good at. Then, start working on your content strategy and become a successful YouTuber.

Creating Your Content Strategy

After deciding your niche and creating your channel, you need to figure out your content strategy. Trust me, without a suitable strategy; you might fail! Let me tell you that your priority should be to create videos that are worth watching and sharing. Well, if viewers don't like your content, they won't share your videos. Eventually, you will not be able to reach a broader audience. Now, I will tell you how you can make a perfect content strategy.

Consistency

You have subscribed to several channels on YouTube, right? Now, think about the most popular creators. What is common about them? Well, they keep consistency in their YouTube channel. You need to create a plan and figure out how many videos you will upload each week. One of the most popular content creators on

YouTube, PewDiePie, upload videos daily, and on the other hand, David Dobrik is a famous vlogger who uploads only one or two videos each week. This means that you don't need to upload videos regularly, but you need to be consistent.

Build your community

If you want to grow on YouTube constantly, you will have to create a loyal fanbase. For this purpose, I would suggest that you reply to all comments whenever possible and ask your viewers what they would like to watch. In simple words, you need to communicate and interact with your subscribers. Moreover, reading all comments will help you figure out what type of content your viewers like the most.

Create a series of videos

A great strategy to keep your viewers hooked to your YouTube channel is to create a series of videos. For example, you have a cooking channel. You can create a series of videos on how to cook Chinese food. Big content creators on YouTube utilize this strategy to keep people coming for more content.

Collaborate

In order to gain more subscribers and grow on YouTube, you need to collaborate with other YouTubers. When you collaborate, it helps you to attract the audience of the other YouTuber and vice-versa. Moreover, you can come up with some excellent ideas.

Optimize your content

You are creating amazing videos but still not getting views. Well, some people don't spend time making their videos visible to searchers, and eventually, their videos do not get views. You need to rank higher on YouTube, right? For this purpose, you should use keywords in the title, relevant tags, and an attractive thumbnail. Moreover, a well-crafted description attracts more viewers.

You Must have tools for your channel

After creating a solid content strategy, you need to understand that you should use the best tools for creating videos. You should use powerful video and photo editing software and Google Keyword Planner to find keywords. Moreover, you need to use YouTube Studio to manage your channel.

How YouTubers make money?

After creating a successful YouTube channel, it is time to talk about real business. If you want to qualify for monetization, your channel must have at least one thousand subscribers. Moreover, YouTube requires 4,000 hours of watch time during the past 12 months. Apart from enabling monetization, you can also use your channel to generate traffic to your blog. Moreover, paid sponsorships, affiliates, and merchandise will also help you generate extra income.

The reason behind PewDiePie's success

While there are numerous examples of people who became successful on YouTube, I think PewDiePie's story has some important lessons for you. This man is also known as Felix Arvid Ulf Kjellberg, and he is a Swedish YouTube vlogger. Let me tell you that he didn't become famous due to a viral hit video. Instead, the key to his success is consistency. He regularly uploads videos, and when he started getting famous, Felix built upon his success. This indicates that there is no secret formula to becoming successful on YouTube. It requires consistency, quality videos, and hard work. Felix also spends a lot of time while discussing the queries of his fans in the comments section.

BONUS SECTION

CHAPTER 11

SELL YOUR SERVICES AS A GRAPHIC DESIGNER

Sell your services as a graphic designer

Are you a creative person who finds himself daydreaming about creating designs in your spare time? Let me tell you that becoming a freelance graphic designer might be the best career choice for you. Many people think that they cannot earn

a substantial income as a graphic designer. However, you might want to note that several designers earn thousands of dollars monthly while working from home. One such freelancer is Joana Galvao, who has started her graphic design business. She decided to become a designer at the age of 22 and began with low expectations. This designer was able to earn a revenue of 100K dollars within ten months of going solo. She says that you don't need a ton of cash to transform your life. Although Joana had earned a degree in graphic designer, you can start your career as a graphic designer by taking up a course.

First of all, you need to learn to design, and then start selling your services as a designer. Joana wanted an exciting, flexible lifestyle. As she says, she wanted to be able to work from the beach. Joana watched videos from Coach Marie Forleo. She was inspired and thought of getting freelance clients so that she could quit her boring job. Her first goal was to make 2,000 dollars in ten days to join Marie's marketing course, B-School. Joanna commented on Marie's video, 'Wouldn't it be great if I magically started getting clients. Surprisingly, a woman replied to her comment and said that she could get a log for 800 dollars. Although Joana usually charged 100 dollars for one logo, she played smart and said that normally she charges $1,000, but I can do it for you for $800. After creating a logo for this client, Joana had begun her journey as a successful freelance graphic designer. After two months, Joana quit her job and started focusing on her graphic designing business. Joana says that to get to become a successful entrepreneur, you need to become bigger. Now, we will discuss how you can become a graphic designer and earn thousands of dollars, just like Joana.

Training to become a designer

The first step towards your journey as a successful graphic designer is to start learning. Joana says that you should take as many art & computer classes as you can. If you are in high school, take drawing, photography, and painting schools. Moreover, you can also learn on your own. Just type 'graphic design course' in Google, and download the courses. You can find thousands of tutorials on YouTube, Illustration Guides, and Hack Design. However, a degree or certificate can give you an advantage while you are applying for jobs. Try visiting your local community college and take a graphic design course. Or you can also go for a bachelor's degree in art in graphic design. Regardless, most clients focus on your

skills. So your priority is to become a graphic designer who can offer the best services.

Obtain work experience

Before you go to Fiverr or Upwork to get graphic designing jobs, you should first obtain work experience. For this purpose, you can volunteer your services at a local charity. You can offer to create logos, prints, and banners for non-profit organizations. Although it won't get you any money, you would have enough samples to show to your potential clients. Always remember that your potential clients will prefer to hire you if you have something to show them. Another way to create your work portfolio is to apply for an internship while in college. Now, you have created several logos, banners, and other graphic design materials; it is time to pick your best pieces of work and include them in your portfolio. Don't add everything you have ever created. Try including only those pieces of work that demonstrate your abilities. Moreover, you need to include a variety of examples that showcase the range of your skills. In the end, create a website for your work.

Ways to earn money as a graphic designer

Successful graphic designers like Joana recommend that you should try to make money in several ways instead of focusing on just one or two ways. The most profitable way to get passive income as a graphic designer is to create and sell templates. Start by creating templates for posters, Pinterest graphics, invitations, ebooks and selling them online. Several small businesses and bloggers love purchasing these templates since it is easier to customize them. Once you have set your template shop, you only have to advertise your products. Another way is to sign up for freelancing websites and start selling your services on such platforms. Joana found her first client by commenting on a video, which means that you need to make your online presence and advertise your skills. Apart from getting clients from freelance sites, you might also get them from social media platforms such as Facebook and Twitter. You can join Facebook groups that are created for graphic designers and get potential customers from such groups. Let me tell you that freelancing lets you try various things at your pace and earn money.

One of the most popular freelancer websites is Upwork, which makes it easier for you to connect with clients. On this website, clients post their requirements, and freelancers offer them their services. Other websites such as Freelancer.com and Fiverr also work the same way. Just keep in mind that clients mostly hire designers based on earlier projects that you upload on the website. Linking your social media profiles to your Upwork account is a great way to help this website find the right type of customers for you. It is worth mentioning that if you have become a professional graphic designer, you can also create your course and sell it.

You can share your knowledge through websites such as Pluralsight, Skillshare, and Udemy.

CHAPTER 12

Become A Freelance Writer

Become a freelance writer

You can get paid for writing content. Sounds amazing? Well, if you love writing about something, you can definitely become a freelance writer just like Kate Burnett. She had always wanted to become a professional writer and earn money by writing. In fact, she wanted to establish a business that could give her the freedom to be present with her family. She loves writing, which led her to become a freelance writer. When she started out as a writer, she created two sites in just five days, landed four different clients, and earned 1,600 dollars in the first month. Previously, Kate tried out for several jobs, and she became a mother before deciding to become a freelance writer. When Kate became a mother, her priorities changed, and she could not deal with petty office politics anymore. More than anything, Kate wanted to spend most of her time with her kids. She says that her belief that writers are 'starving artists' was holding her back from starting this successful freelance writing business. It was not easy for her to establish the business. But with consistency, hard work, and dedication, Kate was able to establish her business. Kate says that she was confused about whether to start a blog or a writing business. She eventually ended up building two sites, one for the blog and the other for freelance writing. She decided on a niche and found her first client via an Australian online task bidding website called Airtasker. Now, we will discuss how you can become a successful writer like Kate.

Types of freelance writing

First of all, you need to understand the types of writing. SEO writing, blogging, copywriting, technical writing, and B2B writing are some of the examples of freelance writing. Blogging is also known as content writing, and when we discuss blogging, you think of your favorite marketing blog, right? Well, blogs pay freelance writers to create content. Now, if you want to become a copywriter, you will have to write persuasive content. It involves selling skills since you are writing to make people purchase a specific product.

How to get started

After understanding the types of freelance content writing, you need to know how you will get started. You can start by identifying those skills and topics you already know. I would suggest that you create a list of your skills and see what pops up. Now, start narrowing down and choose your niche. Although you can write on any topic, focusing on one niche will help you get started easily. Ask yourself, if you were asked to pick one topic and write over 1,500 words on it, what would that topic be? However, if you cannot decide your niche, financial services, insurance, technology, hospitality, and health are some of the niches to get started with. The next step is to start your research. Create a list of websites, blogs, and people in your niche, and analyze them. Now you need to start thinking about your target clients and where to find them.

How to get work

You can write great content, have decided your niche, and analyzed it; what is the next step? Let me tell you that if you don't have any connection with your potential clients, you cannot make money, right? For this purpose, create your website and use it as a way for people to find out more about you and check your samples. You only have to create a simple website that showcases your skills and some samples. Another way to reach clients is to sign for professional content websites. It involves signing up for the site, posting your samples, and you might get matched with a potential client. Some of the most popular websites for such tasks are Skyword and Contently. You can also find clients through social media or by contacting a marketing agency. Some other websites, such as Fiverr, Upwork, Freelancer, and Guru.com, can help you find potential clients. Here are some other ways to make money as a freelance content writer

Pitch a guest post

Several successful blogs accept guest posts, and many of them pay for those posts. You can find numerous such blogs according to your niche. Don't forget to understand the posting guidelines of that blog, and then make your guest post pitch. If you successfully publish a guest post, you will add a piece of content to your portfolio, some money in your bank account, and you will have a byline on a site.

Start Blogging

Suppose that you are unable to find any clients on those professional websites and social media platforms that couldn't help you reach any client. What will you do now? You can try creating a money-making blog. Moreover, you can develop your audience and style through blogging, which might eventually help you land a customer. One of your readers might get impressed by your writing style and hire you. I would suggest that you also add a 'hire me!' button on your blog, so people can easily contact you if they decide to hire you.

Writing a listicle

Did you know that you can also get paid for writing down a listicle? Can you write the top 10 locations on the planet to visit? Well, you might be surprised to know that websites such as TopTenz and Listverse pay people for top 10 lists. Your job is to figure who is hiring and then start pitching.

Publish your book

Can you write a novel or a collection of essays? If yes, then you can make money by writing and publishing your book on Amazon. Amazon Kindle Direct Publishing helps you publish your book and earn money. Start by uploading the book and marketing your book. Moreover, you can advertise your book on your personal blog. These were some of the ways you can earn money as a freelance content writer. There are still numerous opportunities out there for you. You only have to figure out what is the most convenient way for you to make a substantial income through freelance writing.

CONCLUSION

There are many reasons to start an online business and work towards building an appreciative asset. However, this doesn't necessarily mean it's the right approach for you.

You must consider your situation and goals for yourself. However, if you're interested in long-term profitability or the possibility of future sales, doing business online can be the right approach. And with the right approach, you have the potential to become rich.

Made in the USA
Monee, IL
04 November 2026

67387878R00049